HOPING YOU WIL[L] [BE A]
FREQUENT VISITOR [TO] OUR
FLORIDA VACATION WORLD!

LOVE -

Doug

&

Kathy

JULY, 2006

FLORIDA'S

Copyright © 1992 Brompton Books Corp.

This edition published in 1992
by SMITHMARK Publishers Inc.,
16 East 32nd Street,
New York, New York 10016.

SMITHMARK books are available for bulk purchase
for sales promotion and premium use. For details
write or telephone the Manager of Special Sales,
SMITHMARK Publishers Inc., 16 East 32nd Street,
New York, NY 10016. (212) 532-6600.

Produced by Brompton Books Corp.,
15 Sherwood Place,
Greenwich, CT 06830.

ISBN 0-8317-3233-4

Printed in Hong Kong

10 9 8 7 6 5 4 3 2 1

VACATION WORLD

TEXT   ROBIN LANGLEY SOMMER

DESIGN   ADRIAN HODGKINS

SMITHMARK

3-6 Vacationers on the beach at Daytona.

INTRODUCTION

The attractions of the Florida peninsula, America's subtropical state, are so diverse and unusual that it has become the nation's most popular vacation resort. In a sense, the whole region is a kind of national park. It's easy to see why Ponce de Léon thought he could find the Fountain of Youth here. Florida's endless beaches, azure seas, unclouded skies and warm climate are rejuvenating and produce a profusion of life.

The waters of the Atlantic Ocean off the East Coast and the Gulf of Mexico on the West are filled with schools of fish, and their shores are home to many kinds of birds, from curlews and gulls to the great blue heron and the roseate spoonbill. The state's deep-sea fishing is legendary, and its inland waterways are an invitation to pleasure boating. Luxurious marinas dot both coasts all the way to Key West, making Florida a haven for mariners from around the world. The state's natural attractions have been enhanced and made accessible to everyone who feels the call of this unique vacation world.

At Lake Buena Vista, outside Orlando, is Florida's most popular attraction: the 27,000-acre Walt Disney World Vacation Resort. It began in the late 1960s as an enormous land reclamation project involving thousands of workers, and today it employs thousands more. Artificial lakes, hills, and waterways appeared on the huge site as if by magic. Luxurious hotels arose to house visitors to the world's largest fantasy theme park, the Magic Kingdom. Fireworks blaze by night, and parades add sound and color during the day. Such popular Disney characters as Mickey Mouse, Donald Duck and Pluto throng the streets and greet visitors. Fantasyland, Frontierland, Main Street USA, and lavish stage shows all contribute to the excitement.

In 1982 Walt Disney's dream of an Experimental Prototype Community of Tomorrow (EPCOT) was realized at the EPCOT Center, dominated by the silver sphere called Spaceship Earth. Since then new nations have been added to the World Showcase, centered around a huge lagoon, and a dizzying array of pavilions comprises Future World: The Living Seas, Universe of Energy, Journey into Imagination and more. Backstage Magic shows how the center's sophisticated computer system operates behind the scenes to make it all work.

In 1989 the long-awaited Disney-MGM Studios theme park opened, adding a new dimension to the resort. Movies and their making are the attraction here—from bustling Hollywood Boulevard to the thrills of The Great Movie Ride. The Epic Stunt Spectacular re-creates scenes from such adventure films as *Raiders of the Lost Ark*, complete with fires and plane crashes.

A recent addition to Walt Disney World is Typhoon Lagoon, a 56-acre water adventure park which features ocean-sized waves on the world's largest concrete pool. The lagoon offers surfing; a watershed-mountain ride; Shark Reef, complete with a shipwreck on the seafloor; and Castaway Creek, which circles the lagoon for leisurely viewing from giant inner tubes. Besides its many water sports, Walt Disney World offers golfing at three 18-hole courses, the Magnolia, the Palm, and the Lake Buena Vista, plus tennis at 13 lighted courts scattered around the complex. Boaters can operate catamarans, sunfish, mini-speedboats, paddle boats, and canoes on the Walt Disney World waterways. Biking, jogging trails, and horseback riding are all available.

The extensive Disney Village Marketplace offers merchandise from around the world, and the adjacent Pleasure Island has a variety of night-time entertainment, from Mannequin's Dance Palace to the Neon Armadillo Music Saloon and the Comedy Warehouse.

Luxurious accommodations include Disney's Grand Floridian Beach Resort, in the elegant Victorian style, which overlooks the Seven Seas Lagoon. Its five-story Grand Lobby is domed in stained glass. Five island villages comprise the colorful Disney's Caribbean Beach Resort, centered around the plaza called Old Port Royale, with its calypso music, Spanish fort and fountain. The Disney Village Resort has a variety of airy town-houses, rustic villas and even elegant 'treehouses' in a parklike setting that includes five swimming pools.

One could spend months at Walt Disney World without running out of things to see and do, but central Florida has many other diversions that most visitors want to explore, notably Sea World, Circus World and the Wet 'n' Wild water park, all in and around Orlando. These have appeared in the wake of Walt Disney World, while older attractions such as Winter Haven's Cypress Gardens and the pristine waters of Silver Springs have maintained their appeal. Winter Haven is also the spring training home of the Boston Red Sox. Many major league baseball teams make their spring homes in Florida, and spring training attracts many visitors to Florida every year.

The East Coast, too, has flourished as a vacation mecca since the late 19th century, when Henry Flagler's railroad made it accessible. The state's Spanish heritage is apparent in the stucco mansions, archways, grillwork, and patios of its older sections. St Augustine, the nation's first city, wears its long history well and offers incomparable views of colonial days here. Spiky palmettos, soaring royal palms, and flowering vines grow all along the coast, from Cape Canaveral, site of the John F Kennedy Space Center, to Palm Beach. NASA's huge Vehicle Assembly Building and 10-story Titan missiles dominate the complex called the Space Coast. Rocket and space-shuttle sites project into the Atlantic, launching vehicles that speed down the Eastern Test Range in clear view of area beaches.

Daytona Beach has both action, at the famous Daytona International Speedway, and leisure along more than 20 miles of beachfront. Farther south, West Palm Beach offers a safari through Lion Country and incomparable views of the Atlantic. South Florida hums with the energy of Miami and offshore Miami Beach, whose white sands and luxurious hotels and nightlife have attracted visitors since 1915. Some of them have returned in their retirement years to make 'the Beach' a real community as well as a popular resort. Celebrity homes dot North Bay Drive, and private docks house expensive pleasure boats. Nearby Fort Lauderdale, Hollywood and Dania have grown steadily since the 1950s and are especially popular with boaters.

Over the years the West Coast has evolved from a series of pleasant fishing villages to a Gulf resort of fine bleached sand and tranquil waters, with accommodations for every budget. One of its best-known attractions is Tampa's 300-acre Busch Gardens, which includes one of the nation's finest zoos—the Dark Continent. Live mermaids perform underwater ballets at historic Weeki Wachee Springs, whose river was named by the Indians for its wandering course. In Sarasota, circus history is king, in John Ringling's exotic mansion, C'ad'zan, and the adjacent art museum built with his fortune. The Circus Museum preserves the golden age of 'The Greatest Show on Earth' in colorful memorabilia. Ringling's energy and wealth helped to make Sarasota the cultural capital of the state.

St Petersburg, long known as a placid retirement community, has branched out into tourism, with excellent hotels and restaurants. Its Sunken Gardens are famous for their variety of tropical trees and flowers. South of here are the cities of Fort Myers and Naples, the gateway to the Everglades, a subtropical wilderness nourished by a vast, shallow river that originates in Lake Okeechobee and flows into the Gulf of Mexico.

Visitors may enter the Everglades on the single paved road that runs into its heart, with tributary roads to trails and boardwalks. The Ingraham Highway was constructed by the National Park Service and its various stops and trails provide safe access to the sights of this wilderness area. Long Pine Key has a seven-mile nature trail through the pinelands, and the Anhinga Trail boardwalk offers a view of the large diving bird that is often called the snake bird, a relative of the cormorant. White ibises, red-bellied turtles sunning themselves, and colorful zebra butterflies on tropical blossoms are all part of the Everglades panorama. Less welcome—except to hungry birds and frogs—are the mosquitoes.

Canoers may visit the Everglades via the Noble Hammock Canoe Trail, which winds through mangrove clusters for more than two miles. A more demanding route is the Hell's Bay Trail, which leads five miles deep into uncharted parts of the Everglades. The hundred-mile Wilderness Waterway runs from Everglades City south to the Flamingo Marina, taking in such outposts as Alligator Bay, Big Lostman's Bay, Cabbage Island and the Shark River. The Shark Valley entrance to Everglades National Park has a winter-season tram ride through the saw-grass prairie to an observation tower from which visitors can see and hear dozens of alligators splash and bellow.

As one views the ever-changing colors and life forms of the great river of grass, it is not hard to believe that the Everglades evolved over six million years of shifting sea action and limestone build-up beneath the Florida peninsula. It is fortunate that so much of this fragile natural treasure has been preserved for generations to come.

Nature and its ways are also the prevailing theme in the Florida Keys, connected to the mainland south of Miami by the Overseas Highway. Off Key Largo is the nation's first underwater park, John Pennekamp Coral Reef State Park, which takes in 78 square miles of living reef. Scuba diving, snorkeling and glass-bottom boat trips give access to a world of delicate, multicolored coral formations and over 650 species of dazzling tropical fish. Here, too, are the queen or horseshoe conchs that give Key West dwellers their nickname. These giant sea snails, with their handsome spiral shells, are prized by both collectors and cooks. Conch fritters, chowder and salad are staples of island menus, along with the delicious Key Lime pie made from tiny limes that grow wild throughout the region.

Sport fishermen from around the world come to Upper and Lower Matecumbe Keys, and Islamorada—Spanish for 'purple isle.' The evocative name was given by an explorer who saw masses of violet sea snails along the shoreline. A small armada of deep-sea fishing vessels plies nearby waters for marlin, tarpon and bonefish, which can also be taken in shallow waters from flat-bottom boats. Sand sharks and manta rays flit across the sea floor only a few feet below—a Sea World in its natural state.

Key West is the last stop on the Overseas Highway: a crossroads of cultures and lifestyles that has its own unique style. 'Sunset' is a nightly celebration on Mallory Pier. Lively night spots and serene architecture with a Caribbean air contribute to the island's ambience. It is just the place to conclude a magical visit to Florida's vacation world.

CENTRAL FLORIDA

The heart of Florida's vacation world is the 43-square-mile Walt Disney World Vacation Resort—the world's top tourist attraction. Twice the size of Manhattan Island, the resort includes three spectacular theme parks—the Magic Kingdom, EPCOT Center, and Disney-MGM Studios—two lakes, three championship golf courses, and more than 16 luxurious hotels.

The newest attraction at Magic Kingdom Park is Mickey's Birthdayland, an ongoing celebration of the great mouse's 60th birthday, which occurred in 1988. A trip on the Walt Disney World Railroad takes you to Mickey's House and Minnie's Kitchen, where Goofy, Donald, Pluto and Chip 'n' Dale are helping to make a cake for the spectacular Mickey's All-American Birthday Parade. The parade's two-story floats and costumed bands travel the length of Main Street USA, with its Federal- and Victorian-style buildings, and wind through Frontierland to the park's centerpiece: Cinderella's Castle. Its gold-crested spires soar 180 feet above the moat, complete with gargoyles and other embellishments modeled on the fairy-tale castles of France and Bavaria. Other attractions of the Magic Kingdom include the Jungle Cruise, Tomorrowland's Space Mountain, Pirates of the Caribbean, Fantasyland and The Haunted Mansion. Favorite rides include the 'runaway' mine train down Frontierland's Thunder Mountain, flying Dumbo, and Peter Pan in the skies over London.

EPCOT Center fulfills a dream of Walt Disney's that was carried out by his successors: the Experimental Prototype Community of Tomorrow, which opened in 1982. Some of EPCOT's visions have already become reality, including complex systems utilizing laser beams, holograms and computers. EPCOT's journey into Future World begins at the gleaming geosphere called Spaceship Earth, 18 stories high. Future World brings visitors to The Living Seas, The Universe of Energy, The World of Motion, and other destinations including an orbiting space station, a desert farming community, and a 'floating city' under the sea.

In EPCOT Center's World Showcase, which rims a huge lagoon, eleven nations can be explored through their food, music and culture. Visitors can lift a stein at Germany's perpetual Oktoberfest, tour China's Temple of Heaven, and sample Moroccan cuisine. The entire complex is lit up with dazzling light pictures in GE's nightly laser display, IllumiNations.

Walt Disney World's third theme park is the Disney-MGM Studios, centered around bustling Hollywood Boulevard. This popular attraction, which opened in 1989, includes 'The Great Movie Ride' through the excitement of classic films, the Epic Stunt Spectacular, The Monster Sound Show, and SuperStar Television. The Backstage Studio Tour offers an inside look at the world of movie production from the Backstage Shuttle, with stops at Catastrophe Canyon, The Special Effects Workshop and The Magic of Disney Animation.

Many historic Central Florida attractions have been rejuvenated by their proximity to Walt Disney World, including crystalline Silver Springs, Cypress Gardens, and Bok Tower Gardens in Lake Wales. New vacation spots have sprung up around Orlando since Walt Disney World opened, making this one of the fastest growing metropolitan areas in the nation. At Sea World, you can see a killer whale perform, watch penguins and seals, and follow a tunnel through a poolful of sharks. At Universal Studios Florida, visitors quake before the 30-foot-tall King Kong, pedal a Star Bike with ET, and take a ride Back to the Future. Water parks abound, including Wet 'n' Wild, with its 400-foot slides, wave-making pool and Raging Rapids inner-tube ride. From fairy-tale castles to forays beneath the seas, Central Florida is no place like home.

15 A spectacular fireworks display illuminates Cinderella's Castle, Walt Disney World.

16-17 Alice in Wonderland, the Mad Hatter, and the White Rabbit stand in a gazebo while tourists flock over the bridge to Cinderella's Castle in the background.

18 Mickey and Minnie Mouse wave to the
crowd as a parade winds down Main Street.

19 A horse-drawn trolley, which rides down
Main Street USA, is a delightful way to tour the
Magic Kingdom.

20 The Dumbo flying elephant ride is a favorite
with adults and children alike.

21 Pluto hugs a couple of his new pals.

22 The whirling Tea Cup Ride at dizzying top speed.

23 Buoyant Mickey balloons brighten a day at the Magic Kingdom.

24 *In Fantasyland, Captain Nemo's submarine travels to 20,000 Leagues Under the Sea.*

25 *The Big Thunder Mountain Railroad streaks through Frontierland.*

26-27 *Gleaming Spaceship Earth ushers you into the future at EPCOT Center.*

*28 A streamlined monorail cruises through
EPCOT Center into tomorrow.*

29 The Living Seas pavilion in EPCOT's Future World has the world's largest saltwater tank, holding 5½ million gallons.

30-31 EPCOT's World Showcase: The entrance to the China pavilion frames a replica of Peking's Temple of Heaven.

32 The Middle East comes to life at the
Morocco pavilion in EPCOT's World Showcase.

33 A German town in EPCOT's World
Showcase, where visitors can tour 11 nations
without a passport.

34 At the Disney-MGM Studios Theme Park,
Hollywood magic creates a storm at sea.

35 Crowds throng to the exciting Hollywood
Boulevard at Disney-MGM Studios.

36-37 The Indiana Jones stunt show at Disney-
MGM Studios' Epic Stunt Spectacular.

38-39 Water slide thrills at Disney World's River
Country.

40 Disney's elegant Grand Floridian Beach
Resort recalls the golden age of travel.

41 The glittering Victorian lobby of Disney's
Grand Floridian Beach Resort.

42-43 Bright colors and calypso themes reign
at Disney World's Caribbean Beach Resort.

44 The Empress Lilly, *a double-decker riverboat, has three restaurants.*

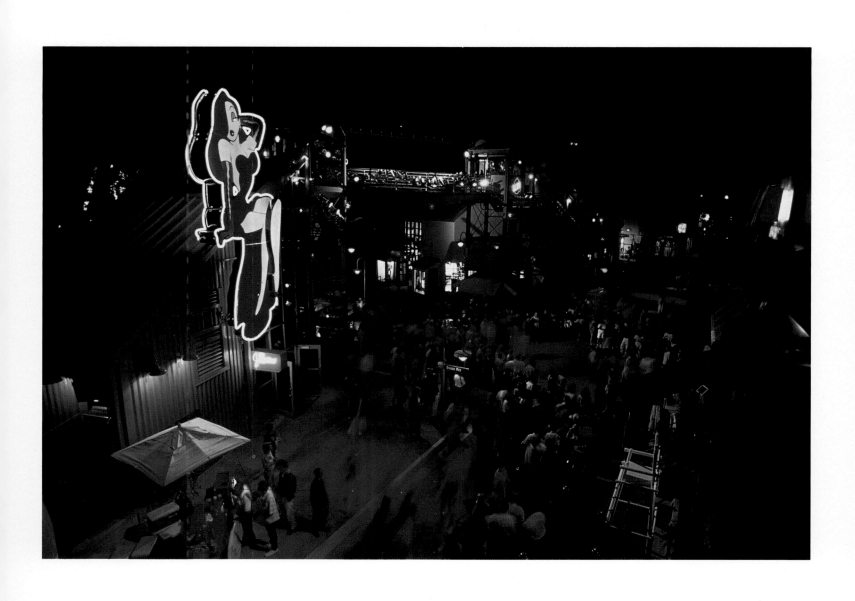

*45 Disney's Pleasure Island, a cluster of
nightclubs, restaurants and shops.*

46 Orlando's Sea World proves that killer whales are anything but scary.

47 Feeding the dolphins is one of Sea World's biggest attractions.

48 Water-skiers, dressed as superheroes in this scene, put on an amazing show at Sea World every day.

49 A set for the classic 'Happy Days' television series at Universal Studios, Florida.

50 The fall Mums Festival clothe beautiful
Cypress Gardens in a mantle of many colors.

51 A trip to Orlando isn't complete without a
run from the slide tower at Wet 'n' Wild water
park.

THE EAST COAST

Most of Florida's 400-year history is along the East Coast, starting at St Augustine, the first permanent settlement by Europeans in the continental United States. St Augustine calls itself the nation's oldest city, and a wealth of evidence backs up that claim. Zorayda Castle, modeled on Granada's Alhambra, and Old St Augustine, with its narrow brick streets and Spanish houses, preserve the city's origins. The historic fortress of Castillo de San Marcos overlooks Matanzas Bay, where the Bridge of Lions stretches to Anastasia Island.

At Daytona Beach, 23 miles of firm, flat sand make it possible to drive right down the waterfront—at a sedate 10 miles per hour. Before 1959 the beach was the site of international auto racing by such drivers as Barney Oldfield and Sir Malcolm Campbell, who broke five records here. But as race cars got faster and the crowds increased, motor sports moved to Daytona International Speedway. Daytona's many attractions have also made it popular with college students on spring break, who once flocked mainly to Fort Lauderdale.

The John F Kennedy Space Center at Cape Canaveral is a huge monument to the American space program. Here visitors can experience simulated flight in pressurized cabins and tour the hangars that house the enormous rockets. Adjacent to the space center is the Merritt Island National Wildlife Refuge, where some 250 species of birds nest and winter. Offshore waters swarm with game fish, including trout and snook.

South of here, luxurious Palm Beach beckons the rich and famous. Fort Lauderdale has grown steadily in size and beauty from its obscure origins as a military outpost in the 1850s. Not only college students, but visitors of every age are drawn to the city's hotels, boating facilities and miles of scenic waterways that gave it the nickname 'Venice of America.' Night clubs attract capacity crowds every weekend, and the 35-acre Bahia Mar marina is crowded with luxurious yachts.

Once a palmetto scrubland on Biscayne Bay, metropolitan Miami and its sister city, Miami Beach, have seen explosive growth, decline and renaissance in less than a hundred years. The fabled Gold Coast sprang to life along the route of Henry Flagler's railroad, with its influx of winter-weary tourists from the North. Latin-flavored downtown Miami has achieved international status as a banking and finance center since 1959, when many wealthy Cubans fled here after Fidel Castro took over their homeland. Their compatriots have been arriving ever since. Street signs, bodegas, popular shrines and nonstop nightlife testify to the presence and energy of the Cuban community. Tourism is still vital to Miami's economy, and the city is the world's busiest port for luxurious cruise ships. Pleasure boating and fishing are pursued avidly, both by visitors and year-round residents.

Early in the 20th century, Miami Beach was a long sandspur off Miami, choked with tropical vegetation. Developer Carl Fisher used circus elephants to cut Lincoln Road through dense stands of mangrove. By the 1930s, 'the Beach' was covered with stylish Art Deco hotels, turquoise pools and lavish mansions visited during the winter months but maintained year-round by large staffs of servants. Collins Avenue became the main artery, and causeways connected the resort city to Miami. Miami Beach was the dream destination of the nation, and during the 1950s, huge hotels such as the Fontainebleau and the Eden Roc took their place in the sun. Many longtime visitors retired here, to modest hotels and boardinghouses on the South Beach. No matter where you go on the scenic East Coast, from historic St Augustine to the Art Deco district of Miami Beach, there is something to admire and enjoy.

54 Old St Augustine preserves the Spanish colonial ambience of the nation's first city.

53 In Fort Lauderdale, every weekend feels like the Fourth of July.

55 The historic red-roofed church and bell tower in Old St Augustine.

56 High-banked Daytona International Speedway is reputed to be the world's fastest track.

57 Vehicles headed for Daytona's fishing pier are limited to speeds of 10 miles per hour on the beach's hard-packed sand.

58-59 The John F Kennedy Space Center at Cape Canaveral.

60 The space shuttle Discovery poised for take-off.

61 The lighthouse commanding Ponce de Léon Inlet at New Smyrna Beach, near Cape Canaveral.

62 Croquet on the manicured lawn of Palm Beach's oldest luxury hotel, The Breakers.

63 Wealthy Palm Beach is one of the world's best known resort communities.

64-65 The Boca Hotel and Club at Boca Raton is famous for its opulent loggias, tiled patios and sculptured fountains.

66 Fort Lauderdale started out as a military
outpost in 1857; now it is known as the Venice
of America.

67 Sunbathing and water sports are a way of
life in relaxed Fort Lauderdale.

68-69 Miami Beach has rebounded to its
former place in the sun after a hiatus of several
decades.

70 An enterprising runner has the sunrise all to
herself.

71 A welcome respite from winter has brought
visitors to Miami Beach since 1915.

72 The formal gardens at Vizcaya overlook
beautiful Biscayne Bay.

73 The island resort of Key Biscayne, with
Miami's skyline in the background.

*74 The Art Deco district of Miami Beach
preserves the 1930s style of the city that called
itself 'the sun and fun capital of the world.'*

75 More than 800 Art Deco buildings went up
around Miami Beach's Flamingo Park, and
many of them have been handsomely
refurbished as National Historic Places.

76 Wealthy celebrity residents such as
comedian Jackie Gleason helped restore
Miami Beach to its former eminence as a
haunt of the rich and famous.

77 The grandiose facades along Miami
Beach's Collins Avenue give it the look of a
movie set.

78-79 Color is a building block of Miami
architecture.

80 Miami's exotic Parrot Jungle draws visitors
from around the world.

81 Shell-pink flamingos at rest remind one of
Alice in Wonderland.

82-83 Multicultural Miami lights up the night
along Biscayne Bay.

THE WEST COAST

The Gulf of Mexico washes the fine sand of the long West Coast, which has been developing into a popular resort area since railroad-builder Henry B. Plant extended his South Florida Railroad to Tampa in 1884. Today Tampa is the site of 300-acre Busch Gardens, with its African theme park, The Dark Continent. It attracts more visitors than any other Florida theme park except Walt Disney World and Sea World. Zebras, giraffes, tigers and elephants roam free and have flourished in the park setting. The amusement park offers such thrilling rides as the Python, the Mamba and the Scorpion.

Across Tampa Bay is serene St Petersburg, with its picturesque bay-front and colorful Sunken Gardens. Gulf waters are unusually calm, sometimes mirrorlike on a humid summer day, and boating is a way of life here. The old West Coast still lingers in fishing villages around Cedar Key and enclaves south of Naples.

Cultural Sarasota bears the imprint of circus master John Ringling, who used his elephants to fashion the city to his taste. Its street patterns and Italian statuary are Ringling hallmarks dating back to the 1920s, when Ringling imported tapestries and art from all over the world for his 68-acre estate, C'ad'zan. Eventually, his art collection became so extensive that he built an imposing museum modeled on a Florentine villa. Another museum houses the circus collection, with its colorful memorabilia, posters and calliopes.

Seashells abound on Sanibel Island, where the tides cast up thousands of shells highly prized by collectors, including the rare royal Florida miter and spiny oyster. The wildlife refuge here, named for journalist and environmentalist J N Darling, has a five-mile drive from which to view the many sea and marsh birds that frequent Sanibel and nearby Captiva Island.

Like Central Florida, the West Coast has many clear springs and rivers that offer a host of diversions. Tarpon Springs grew up on the Anclote River, and Weeki Wachee Spring was named by the Indians for the 'winding waters' of its river. The famous mermaids of the spring evolved from an underwater show staged by Navy frogman Newton Perry that grew into a famous attraction. Now professional choreographers and costumers orchestrate the shows.

Inventor Thomas A Edison built a winter estate in Fort Myers in 1886. The Edison Winter Home and Museum houses the products of his Florida laboratory, where he perfected phonographs, motion pictures and the teletype, among other inventions. The estate has extensive tropical gardens, with some 6000 species collected by Edison, including calabash trees from South America.

Naples is a sparkling, well-planned community whose avenues end at unspoiled Gulf beaches. The thousand-foot-long pier is a favored spot with fishermen. The African Safari Park in the Caribbean Gardens features animals collected from around the world by 'Jungle' Larry Tetzlaff.

On Marco Island the quiet old villages of Marco and Goodland, with their modest cottages, recall memories of an older Florida. Calusa Indians lived here 2500 years ago, and their artifacts have been found on archeological digs in the vicinity. South of Marco Island is the network of tiny keys known as the Ten Thousand Islands. West of it, the Big Cypress Swamp meets the Everglades.

85 A fantasy city of sand rises on Cortez Beach, along the Gulf of Mexico.

Banner text (left to right):

JAPANESE
ART

30th
Anniversary

Sister City
Program

TAKAMATSU
&
ST. PETERSBURG

FIGURES FROM LIFE:
PORCELAIN SCULPTURE
FROM THE
METROPOLITAN MUSEUM
OF ART
1740-1780
through April 26

HIDDEN TREASURES
SELECTIONS FROM
THE CORNELL FINE ARTS
MUSEUM
ROLLINS COLLEGE
through May 10

RODIN
BRONZES
FROM THE
IRIS AND B. GERALD
CANTOR
FOUNDATION

Sponsored By
SAM & LORRAINE
RAHALL

86 The imposing Museum of Fine Arts in St Petersburg.

87 Sarasota's Ringling Museum, modeled on a 15th-century Florentine villa, houses a treasure trove of art collected by John Ringling of circus fame.

88-89 The Cincinnati Reds take the field at Plant City Stadium, their spring training headquarters.

90-91 Amusement park rides at Tampa's 300-acre Busch Gardens, which has seven major areas, including one of the country's best zoos.

92 Peaceful Captiva Island is frequented by birds from the wildlife refuge on nearby Sanibel.

93 Campers stake their claim on a piece of the serene Gulf Coast.

94 Pleasure boating off Longboat Key.

95 Children make the most of the West Coast's
bleached sand and clear waters.

96-97 Brown pelicans congregate on a dock in
Bradenton Beach.

98 Mermaids are a common sight at crystalline
Weeki Wachee Spring, home also to exotic
birds, river cruises and the Enchanted Rain
Forest.

99 The Dolphin Theater is a major attraction at
Tampa's Busch Gardens.

100 An extremely rare white tiger: The Dark
Continent theme park, Busch Gardens.

101 A patient elephant does his part at the
Caribbean Zoological Gardens in Naples.

102 Shell collectors flock to Sanibel Island, one
of the world's top three sites for shelling, after
Africa's Jeffreys Bay and the Philippine Sulu
Islands.

103 The J N 'Ding' Darling National Wildlife
Refuge on Sanibel Island shelters hundreds of
different sea and shore bird species.

104 A boardwalk through the Corkscrew
Swamp Sanctuary, 11,000 acres of wilderness
near Fort Myers.

105 Sunset over Blind Pass, between Sanibel
and Captiva islands.

THE EVERGLADES AND THE KEYS

The slow-flowing river that the Indians called *Pa-hay-okee*, 'the grassy waters,' originates in 700-square-mile Lake Okeechobee, far north of Everglades National Park. The park encompasses almost half a million acres, or most of Florida's southern tip, comprising a unique landscape of saw grass, island hammocks of hardwood trees, clumps of gnarled mangroves rising from contorted root systems and patches of slash pine and cypress. The web of life within this vast watery world includes almost 300 kinds of birds; 600 species of fish; and adaptable mammals such as the marsh rabbit, white-tailed deer and raccoon.

Amphibians and reptiles perch on blades of grass and rove through mangrove creeks where the crocodile rules. The brackish waters near Florida Bay is the only place in the United States where the ancient taper-snouted reptile is found. Far more common is the ungainly looking alligator, which inhabits the many 'willows'—light-green tails of vegetation filling the deep water around hammocks of hardwood. These islands may rise three feet above water level, and dry mounds of dead vegetation sprout cabbage palms, strangler figs, West Indian mahogany and satin leaf hardwoods. The hammocks are a refuge for Everglades mammals during the high-water season, and a year-round haunt of the alligator.

Where Florida's southern border meets Florida Bay, the Everglades become 'the Backcountry'—a host of little islands called keys, an anglicized version of the Spanish *cayo*. The best known and some of the largest are the 32 islands known as the Florida Keys, stretching from Biscayne Bay to the Dry Tortugas, 86 miles north of Havana. It's hard to get lost in the Keys, because there's only one highway connecting them to the mainland—the Overseas Highway.

The farther one travels into the Keys, the more they exert their spell. By the time visitors reach the Seven-Mile Bridge between Marathon and Bahia Honda (Deep Bay), they have usually succumbed to Keys Disease, or total relaxation. Life is simplified down to a high, clear sky, an endless sweep of azure and turquoise sea, and clean salt air.

Key Largo boasts of having the country's only underwater park—John Pennekamp Coral Reef State Park—where visitors can view rainbow colored tropical fish from glass-bottom boats or swim among them. Wildlife preserves in the Keys include the National Key Deer Refuge, encompassing Big Pine and No Name Keys. Here dimunutive deer related to the Virginia white-tail browse on the shrubbery around freshwater ponds. The Great Heron and Key West National Wildlife Refuges are home to thousands of sea and shore birds, from bobolinks to kingfishers and the brown pelican. Fishermen ply the waters off the Keys in every kind of vessel, from expensive deep-sea fishing charters to flat-bottom boats that cruise the shallows for bonefish.

Land's end is at Key West, where Bahamian, Cuban and nautical elements combine in an easygoing way of life peculiar to the Conchs, as Key West residents call themselves. The island has many pleasures: fiery sunsets viewed from Mallory Pier; Conch houses with spacious verandas trailing pink frangipani blossoms; the historic retreats of Ernest Hemingway, playwright Tennessee Williams, and Haitian-born John James Audubon. A ride on the sightseeing Conch Train offers a sampling of the local legends and color that give the island a special place in Florida's unique vacation world.

107 Mahogany Hammock, Everglades National Park.

108 An aerial view of the immense shallow river of grass the Indians called Pa-hay-okee.

109 A 'Glades alligator on the watch in his swampy domain.

110 Water hyacinths flourish in the countless slow-moving streams of the Everglades.

111 Walkways and observation posts provide a safe view of the subtropical wilderness.

112 Anhinga and young, members of the cormorant family.

113 The majestic great blue heron in breeding plumage.

114 A white-tail doe alert to danger in her Everglades habitat.

115 Blooms of the mangrove tree.

116-117 The marine wonderland of John Pennekamp Coral Reef State Park, near Key Largo.

118 The Seven Mile Bridge links Marathon Key and Bahia Honda Key.

119 Windsurfers find their element among the Keys.

120 *The gentle manatee, or sea cow, is an endangered animal. The Everglades is home to more plants and animals facing potential extinction than any other national park.*

121 *Captain Tony's Saloon was once Sloppy Joe's Bar, a frequent haunt of Ernest Hemingway.*

122 *At Hemingway House, Key West, such literary masterpieces as A Farewell to Arms were created in the Pool House study.*

123 *Audubon House dates from the early 1800s; its period furnishings include antiques rescued from sinking ships by Key West wreckers.*

CAPT. TONY'S SALOON

COLD PEPERMINT SCHNAPPS $1.00

...d ORIGINAL *SLOPPY JOE'S BAR* IN KEY WEST"
1933~1937

THE FIRST AND ORIGINAL
"SLOPPY JOE'S BAR"
IN KEY WEST, FLA.
1933~1937

TAXI

124 Seashells are big business on congenial
Mallory Square, Key West.

125 Sunset is a high-spirited ritual on Mallory
Pier.

126-127 Safe harbor at land's end.